BE LIKE TREES

An indispensable role in helping Humans create a better future

FREEDOM MARTINS

Table of contents

INTRODUCTION

CHAPTER ONE

TAKE CARE OF YOURSELF FIRST
STAY GROUNDED NO MATTER HOW SUCCESSFUL
SPEND TIME IN SILENCE

CHAPTER TWO

REMEMBER THAT CHALLENGES ARE HERE TO MAKE YOU STRONGER
EMBRACE HUMBLE BEGINNINGS
CONTINUE TO GROW EVEN WHEN LEFT ALONE WITH LIMITED RESOURCES

CHAPTER THREE

SO AS NOT TO LOSE TO THE LIMIT
HAVE A HEART LIKE A TREE AND LEARN TO APPRECIATE THOSE WHO HAVE HELPED YOU ALONG THE WAY

CHAPTER FOUR

LEARN TO ENJOY EVERY MOMENT OF LIFE
YOU HAVE IMMENSE POWER

CHAPTER FIVE

LET GO OF PERFECTIONISM

Happiness comes from within

CHAPTER SIX

Be patient - good things will come
How strong are your roots and value system?
Trees make the world an imaginative and delightful place
Live life wisely and allow others to make the most of their wisdom and virtues

CHAPTER SEVEN

Conclusion

INTRODUCTION

Life on Earth would be unthinkable without trees. They have thrived for millions of years and have helped us evolve into the smartest creatures on earth. Not only are they the key to our existence, but they also teach us valuable life lessons. Face challenges with courage. Steal happiness at any time of the year. Hold on to pain and loneliness. Live happily no matter what happens. Take steady steps, be smart and steady and rise to the top of the world.

CHAPTER ONE

Take care of yourself first

The tree teaches us that we must take care of ourselves first in order to take care of others. Because trees take care of themselves, they have much to offer others, including life-sustaining oxygen, food, resources, and shelter. For example, if a tree does not care for itself by absorbing water and sunlight, it is not strong, healthy, or beautiful enough to offer something of value to others. Therefore, it is important to take care of yourself first, as you cannot pour from an empty cup.

Stay grounded no matter how successful

Another important life lesson you can learn from the tree is to stay grounded and connected to your inner being. The taller and bigger the tree, the deeper its roots grow. Strong ground helps trees withstand high winds without uprooting them. The roots of a tree represent the inside or inside, and the tree itself represents the outside. So grounding means connecting deeply with your inner self. Your inner reality is as important as your outer reality. No matter what happens in the outside world, your inner reality is always silent. When you lose touch with your inner reality, you can easily get lost in the ever-ephemeral, ephemeral outer reality and lose yourself. As Ralph Waldo Emerson rightly said, "What's behind us and ahead of us are minor problems compared to what's inside us."

Spend time in silence

The trees teach us that there is a time to "do" and a time to "be". Life has its ups and downs, ups and downs are full of energy and motivation, while downs are for rest, relaxation, and contemplation. Whenever possible, try to spend time alone by sitting still, asking questions, thinking, and understanding. Contemplation can provide valuable insights for moving on to your next life phase.

CHAPTER TWO

Remember that challenges are here to make you stronger

Another important life lesson that trees teach us is that challenges are here to make you stronger. Trees that are constantly exposed to storms grow stronger and develop deeper roots. You may despise the challenges of life, but when you look back on your life, you will realize that it was the challenges that shaped and made you who you are today. You learn important life lessons by dealing with challenges. You grow internally so that you can reach your true potential. So always keep this in mind whenever you face challenges.

Embrace humble beginnings

Even the tallest trees are not afraid to grow from humble beginnings. Tall, tall, stout and strong oaks were once little acorns. We're all a little weirdos, and it's often a little annoying at first. But it is from humble and chaotic beginnings that we evolve as infinite superior minds, with a pure desire to grow in the face of overwhelming enemy forces. Trees teach us to have a "never give up" attitude in the most hopeless and chaotic times. Surrender yourself to a quest for wisdom to grasp the truth. Have the courage to fight the hardest blows. Develop a brave heart, strive and stumble, but stand up and be ready to win.

Continue to grow even when left alone with limited resources

Trees grow one by one in the most desolate areas, living their talented lives to the fullest. They grow in ocean depths, deserts, mountain peaks, and extreme weather conditions. There are times in our lives when we have to fight alone. Even the closest and dearest people turn their backs on us and leave us alone. Trees teach us to believe in ourselves and keep growing whatever we have. It said: Instead of gleaning enthusiasm from adversity, your conscience will approve only positive actions, all of which will be reflected in your brave self and you will continue to grow."

CHAPTER THREE

So as not to lose to the limit

A tree has to fight external dangers and enemies all its life. Storms break branches, damage roots, and other parts, tear leaves and crush them to death. Yet they age and shine with a more mature glow. Yet they are blue at heart, overwhelmed by peace, and wise in silence. They are exposed to serious injuries throughout their lives. They fight droughts, avalanches, disease, thousands of storms, storms, and floods by standing still. They show us the empowering essence of life and teach us strategies for fighting and winning against tyrants. Never,

never, never give up has to be something special. Give it a try and you will surely experience the heavenly joy of living in a dream world.

Have a heart like a tree and learn to appreciate those who have helped you along the way

Trees selflessly love us, grow, fight adversity, and devote their lives to serve the humanity that planted them...but instead of expressing gratitude, they subtly omit it. They are one of the greatest resources of Divine Mother Earth, the most benevolent and loyal to society. They provide shelter, good food, and beautiful lives, purify the air to give us fresh energy, and teach us wise lessons to live happy and motivated lives. Serving humanity in any way we can, but only giving back our only help in seeding them. I no longer felt the pain of ripping it apart, no longer heard its cries as I cut it down, and no longer heard some of the joy when the wind was strong.

CHAPTER FOUR

Learn to enjoy every moment of life

Trees are perfect for stealing the joy of life. They steal the sun's rays, wet the hearty silver raindrops, tremble as the wind blows, dance in the glorious summer, and in the spring they spin, weave, and throw their branches with glorious tenacity. Your happiness never stops in the face of life's difficulties and the song of life never ends.

You have immense power

Trees teach us that the most mundane things have immense potential, but it takes the right vision to reveal it. The whole tree is hidden inside, even if the seeds seem small and meaningless. Growing a tree from seed only requires the right resources such as soil, water, and sunlight. Recognize that, like a seed, you have immense potential dormant within you. Getting in touch with the right resources can help them thrive. These resources include the right attitude, the right vision, self-confidence, and self-awareness.

CHAPTER FIVE

Let go of perfectionism

The really important life lesson that trees teach us is that perfectionism is an illusion. Wood is never perfect, but it is beautiful. In fact, their beauty comes from imperfection. You can never be perfect because perfection is inherently subjective. What looks perfect to one person may not look perfect to another. Whenever you try to be perfect, you are trying to achieve the unattainable. For this reason, perfectionism stifles creativity and prevents us from taking action and expressing our true selves. So don't waste your time striving for perfection. We will try our best, but don't worry about doing it perfectly.

Happiness comes from within

You don't need a reason to be happy. Everywhere you look you can find happiness in the simplest things. For example, you can be happy just by focusing your attention on the present moment and developing gratitude for everything. Ten Small actions lead to big changes

Trees teach us that small actions lead to big changes. A goal may seem overwhelming, but with small, steady steps, it will eventually be achieved.

CHAPTER SIX

Be patient - good things will come

The tree reminds us that everything in life happens at the right time and good things always come to those who wait. The tree knows this and does not fight or struggle for it, it simply remains in its existence. When all the leaves fall off in the fall, the tree waits patiently for spring to regenerate. When the land dries up, the trees wait patiently, knowing that it will rain one day. Faith and perseverance are two of the greatest virtues you can have. Because these two virtues will help you face almost anything you face in life.

How strong are your roots and value system?

Trees have very strong and wide root systems. Trees like mesquite have a wide root system, reaching hundreds of feet below ground to reach water sources and touching the sky to grow taller and stronger. Your success and your wisdom in life depend on your roots. It depends on how extensive your system is and how solid your principles are. Are they firmly embedded in your values to guide and illuminate you in making the most important decisions?

Short trees with weak roots are destined to die

Some trees grow rapidly by nature's laws and never grow by strong desire. It cannot grow its branches toward the sun, which is the essence of life, nor can it grow its roots deep into the earth. As a result, they die early without leaving a trace. Young and small trees must grow, drawing inspiration from big, strong, old trees.

Don't let people with low self-esteem, small dreams, lazy desires, and short-sighted people wander around you

They themselves are small, so how can they help extend their reach even further?

Trees make the world an imaginative and delightful place

They are the essence of our existence. They heal our aching tempers, our dull days, our complex, chaotic and boring lives, and embellish and enhance the landscapes around us with their majestic and eternally refreshing beauty. We can also nurture and nurture our inner beauty to make the world around us the most beautiful place. How beautiful would the world be if we weren't focused on spreading love, spreading wisdom, and helping others realize their dreams? We have a life without guarantees, but there are ways to make the most of it by making the planet a happier place for generations to come, if not for ourselves.

Have you ever found yourself hiding under a tree? Not only does it provide a restful night's rest, but it also coordinates everything into a great state of mind, entertaining and serving guests. It offers the breeze of leaves, the sweet scent of flowers, and quiet time, offering perfect relaxation.

Live life wisely and allow others to make the most of their wisdom and virtues

After years of serving us, trees die, leaving useful bodies that can be used for a number of reasons. The leaves rot and provide minerals to other trees in the area, and the forest is used to build housing and furniture. Telling us to leave our virtues behind so that we can.

CHAPTER SEVEN

Conclusion

Trees dig their roots deep into the earth and spread them over a wide area. Roots are often invisible, but they keep the tree grounded as they continually grow through nutrient-rich soil. Thus, roots also need to be buried. The closest network of family and friends nourishes you (both mentally and in the form of delicious sandwiches), helps you grow, and allows you to stay grounded in your life. Forgive yourself for being constant, but don't be afraid to push your roots further. There is always more world to discover.

www.ingramcontent.com/pod-product-compliance
Lightning Source LLC
LaVergne TN
LVHW020539160826
845677LV00015B/4145

* 9 7 9 8 8 4 8 5 2 1 2 0 7 *